# Bridal *Flowers*

RYLAND
PETERS
& SMALL
LONDON NEW YORK

# Bridal *Flowers*

Jane Durbridge

with text by Antonia Swinson

Photography by Craig Fordham

*For Stephen, Mark and Claire, with love.*

**Design** Gabriella Le Grazie and Vicky Holmes
**Commissioning editor** Annabel Morgan
**Location research manager** Kate Brunt
**Production** Patricia Harrington
**Art director** Gabriella Le Grazie
**Publishing director** Alison Starling

**Text** Antonia Swinson

**Hair and makeup** Debbie Warren
**Models** Shona Bingham and Kate Mahoney at
Select; Jo Blyth, Suneetha Goring and Lucy Simmons

**Jane Durbridge can be contacted at:**
janedurbridge@parterre-flowers.co.uk

First published in the United Kingdom in 2002
by Ryland Peters & Small
Kirkman House
12-14 Whitfield Street
London W1T 2RP
www.rylandpeters.com
10 9 8 7 6 5 4 3 2 1

ISBN 1 84172 277 4

A CIP record for this book is available from
the British Library.

Printed and bound in China

# Contents

# *Introduction*

I have a passion for flowers. At the age of four, I was caught picking flowers from the rock garden next to my nursery school to present to my teacher. Later, my father gave me a little plot in our garden where I grew nemesia and cornflowers. At eighteen, I went to Paris as an au pair to learn French. I spent my spare time gazing longingly into the windows of the chic flower shops that dotted the smartest *arrondissements*. It was then that I knew I wanted to work with flowers.

I became a florist, working first for other companies, then setting up my own, Parterre Flowers. Flowers excite and delight me to this day, and arranging flowers for weddings is one of the most rewarding aspects of my job. Once upon a time, white was the traditional choice for bridal flowers, but now anything goes and colour is invariably the starting point when I'm discussing flowers with a bride. That's why I've arranged this book into colour themes, focusing first on colours used alone, then on colour combinations. You'll find bouquets, posies, baskets, hoops, garlands, floral balls and headdresses for the bride and bridesmaids as well as ideas for buttonholes. Some ideas are so simple that anyone could make them, but the majority are best left to the professionals.

When I started out, wedding bouquets were normally wired – a fiddly and time-consuming process. Nowadays, a more natural approach is popular, and the bouquets and posies in this book are mostly hand tied – only the headdresses, hoops and floral balls are wired. I love foliage, seed heads, fruits, twigs, catkins and berries every bit as much as flowers and never regard them as a mere backdrop. Ribbons and fabric also play a starring role in my work – they add a wonderful finishing touch. I find inspiration in many places: flowers in the market, travels abroad, paintings and gardens. Even a scrap of glorious ribbon can be the starting point for a bouquet.

There's greater scope for creativity with wedding flowers than ever before, and brides are becoming increasingly adventurous in their choices. I've had lots of fun letting my imagination run wild during the making of this book. I hope you have as much fun reading it, and find it a rich source of inspiration.

*choosing your flowers*

# the power of flowers

One of the things that marks out a wedding as being such a special celebration is the use of flowers. They're a glorious finishing touch, a way of lifting the day out of the ordinary and into the realms of fantasy. The fact that their natural beauty is transient, designed to last just for one day, also heightens their allure.

Flowers offer us a powerful sensory experience, appealing to our sight, touch and smell, and they have been valued for these qualities for thousands of years. Many civilizations have endowed flowers with powerful symbolism, linking them with fertility and spiritualism. In ancient Greece, custom dictated that brides wore wreaths of flowers, leaves and grains to their marriage ceremonies. The Romans regarded roses as sacred to Venus, the goddess of love, and sprinkled their fragrant petals upon a couple's marriage bed.

In the early eighteenth century, the wife of the British ambassador to Constantinople introduced to England the Turkish custom of assigning sentiments to different flowers. The so-called 'language of flowers' was popularized by the Victorians, who used this romantic code to convey messages of love and affection that decorum demanded should not be voiced openly.

For the modern bride, carrying and wearing flowers is still an unashamedly romantic gesture, a part of her wedding day that she will remember long after the blooms have faded.

far left *A grand dress deserves equally grand flowers. This shower bouquet of pale pink roses and lilies is essentially formal and traditional, although tying rather than wiring the flowers creates a more modern effect.*
left *This ribbon-tied sheaf of sculptural arum lilies would be ideal for a chic contemporary wedding.*
below *Beautiful and long lasting, roses are, not surprisingly, the number one wedding flower. They're also very versatile and look at home at both formal and more relaxed celebrations.*

# choosing a style

A wedding is a natural extension of the bride and groom's personalities and styles. Its overall mood will help to determine the flowers you choose, so before you start to think about your flowers in detail, consider whether your wedding will be traditional or modern, formal or casual, urban or rustic in feel. There are no hard and fast rules, and even if you're marrying in a busy city, you may want to carry a bouquet of cottage-garden flowers. However, in order for your wedding not to be a jumble of disparate themes, it helps if you look at it as a whole, so that you can coordinate important elements such as the dress, the attendants' outfits, the cake and, of course, the flowers.

Colour is the easiest way to do this – there is, after all, nothing more chic than a white wedding. However, there are also many other sources of inspiration. Historical influences might come into play – perhaps you love

Victorian favourites such as lily of the valley and orange blossom. Conversely, your tastes may be uncompromisingly modern, leading you towards dramatic plants such as arum lilies. If your wedding is to be formal, a grand bouquet of roses and lilies is likely to appeal, while for a casual and low-key celebration, a loose posy of wild flowers might fit the bill.

Different times of year can also suggest a theme – a bouquet of orange roses, berries, fruits and leaves, for example, would be ideal for an autumn wedding. Scent may be important to you, causing you to choose a posy of aromatic herbs or delicately fragranced sweet peas. Another important consideration for the bride is her dress, as the bouquet should echo its shape and style. The bride's height and shape should also come into play – for instance, a neat posy will flatter a petite bride more than an enormous bouquet, which could look awkward or overwhelming.

Whatever thoughts you have about the style of your wedding, this is not an occasion for trying to be someone you're not – you'll simply feel uncomfortable. Let the day be a true reflection of your personality, and everything else will follow.

*opposite above left Orange freesias and yellow narcissi are sharpened up with lime-green lady's mantle, making for a zesty colour scheme.*
*opposite above right A vibrant bouquet of tangerine and hot pink ranunculus, lilac and violet sweet peas and white-and-pink camellias.*
*opposite below left Opposites attract: black-red roses contrast dramatically with lime-green guelder rose.*
*opposite below right Using a flower of a single colour is another way to create impact, as demonstrated by this tight posy of shocking pink ranunculus.*
*right Harmonious combinations can be livened up by offsetting a pale shade of one colour with a deeper version of another – here, sky-blue and royal-purple pansies.*
*below right Pastel colours, such as the pale pink and soft lilac of these peonies and flag irises, create a dreamy and romantic effect.*

complementaries, and combinations of these are vibrant and exciting – blue and orange, or red and green. Colours that are neighbours – purple and pink, or orange and red, work harmoniously together. Mixing darker shades of one colour with paler tints of the other can tone down complementary combinations (rose pink and dark green) or liven up harmonious ones (sky blue and royal purple).

Some colours look at their best during certain seasons. The gentle light of spring suits the acid yellows and soft blues of that season's flowers. Bolder colours stand up well to the strong light of summer, while autumnal light bathes rich yellows and oranges in a flattering glow. In the cool light of winter, strong reds, greens and white look dramatic.

However, all these suggestions are just that; the most important thing is that you choose colours that you love and feel comfortable with.

# working with colour

A skilled florist knows how to use colour to produce effects ranging from the ethereal to the dramatic. Many brides are less confident, however, and need a few guidelines.

White and cream are classic wedding colours and are also the easiest to combine with others. Mixing white or cream with pale colours is easy on the eye, while adding dark colours creates a stronger effect. Using varying tones of a single colour, such as pink, can produce gentle or bold effects, depending on whether the tones are close together or contrasting. The alternative is to combine colours. The colour wheel is used to represent the range of colours in the spectrum and to demonstrate their relationships. The colours opposite one another on the wheel are known as

left *Daffodils are one of the most popular spring flowers. Here, they have been combined with ranunculus, narcissi, spring snowflakes and guelder rose, all in a refreshing palette of white, yellow, cream and green.*

below left *An early summer bunch of country flowers – feverfew and globe flowers – in the sunny and simple combination of yellow and white.*

below centre *Green and white look cool and tranquil in the gentle light of spring. This bouquet combines tulips, kangaroo paw, bupleurum and galax.*

below right *This bouquet of sunflowers and cornflowers is as bright and breezy as a summer's day. Vibrant colour schemes such as this work well in the strong summer light.*

Many flowers are now available all year round, including such favourites as roses, tulips, carnations, African daisies, orchids and lilies. These all come in a wide range of colours and it's very useful for florists to be able to rely on them throughout the year, particularly during the winter months. However, many other flowers have a limited season, among them some of the most beautiful, such as peonies, sweet peas, lilac, lily of the valley, bluebells and camellias.

I like to work with the seasons as much as possible for several reasons. There is a distinctive quality to the natural light at different times of year: gentle in spring, strong in summer, mellow in autumn and cool in winter. Flowers

# working with
# the seasons

look at their best and most at home during their natural flowering period because the light flatters their colours and because they harmonize with other flowers around them. Roses are the one exception to this rule – they are available all year round and always look right at a wedding. However, many plants look incongruous if used out of season – for instance, a bouquet of sweet peas at a winter wedding would introduce a jarring note, while snowdrops wouldn't.

Using flowers when they're naturally in bloom also makes it more likely that your florist will be able to get hold of them and that they will be good value for money. You needn't limit yourself to cut flowers: in winter, for instance, pansies may be easiest to get hold of from garden centres as bedding plants. If you observe the seasons, you may also be able to use garden plants, which will save you money.

But perhaps the best argument for observing the seasons is that each one plays host to a marvellous array of flowers. In spring, there are daffodils, bluebells, primroses, ranunculus and tulips, followed by delphiniums, peonies, sweet peas, roses and cornflowers in summer. Hydrangeas, chrysanthemums and Michaelmas daisies are available in autumn, and in winter, hellebores, amaryllis, snowdrops and jasmine appear. Whatever time of year you decide to get married, make the most of what nature has on offer.

*below left and centre  Burnt oranges, russets and warm browns glow in the mellow light of autumn. This bouquet features seasonal leaves, berries, kumquats, cape gooseberries and roses.*

*below  Ruby reds and forest greens (here provided by velvety roses and glossy galax leaves) are colours traditionally associated with winter. Touches of silver add to the festive effect.*

# working with a florist

Organizing flowers on a large scale and working with a professional florist is a new experience for most brides. Finding the right person for the job requires a little homework. Personal recommendation is the best way to start, so ask friends, relatives and colleagues. Your wedding or reception venue may also be able to help. Alternatively, visit local florists. Ask to see a portfolio of their work and about weddings they've undertaken, and discuss the sort of arrangements you want. Make it clear what your budget is, and ask for a written quote. Before making up your mind, ask yourself a few searching questions: does the florist have an impressive portfolio? Do they have lots of wedding experience? Do they seem professional and efficient? Can you afford them? Are they receptive to your ideas? And, most importantly, do you like their style?

Once you have found a florist you feel happy with, you can begin to make decisions about the flowers, colour scheme and number of arrangements. You may have a clear idea of what you want, but many brides feel confused by the huge range of flowers available. If you need inspiration, browse through magazines and books and show them to your florist. Don't worry if you're unsure about plant names – if you've got a picture of a flower, the florist should be able to identify it for you. Have a good look around the florist's shop, too, and see what catches your eye. The bride's dress and attendants' outfits are often the starting point for flowers, so take along swatches of fabric. Your florist will also need to know what kind of wedding you're having as flowers can evoke myriad moods and styles and must fit in with your vision of the perfect wedding.

*opposite It's not impossible to do your wedding flowers yourself, but there are so many other things to think about that most brides turn to a professional. Remember that the more complicated arrangements, such as wired bouquets, floral balls and garlands, will be more expensive than hand-tied bouquets.*
*this page, right and far right The raw materials of the florist's art – the flowers themselves, plus pins and ribbons to tie and embellish them.*
*below right Although they're small, buttonholes are an important finishing touch and can be treated in all sorts of different ways to give them a distinctive look.*

You will then have to decide how many arrangements you want and what they'll consist of. Bear in mind that some will be more expensive than others. Wired bouquets, headdresses and floral balls are fiddly and time-consuming to prepare, and are therefore more expensive than tied bouquets or posies. Flowers vary in price, too. Roses, tulips, lilies and carnations, for example, are available all year round and therefore offer good value for money. Other flowers, such as lily of the valley, peonies and sweet peas, are more seasonal and thus more costly if you are hoping to use them out of season. However, if you've set your heart on something only to find that it's out of your price range, take heart – your florist should be able to suggest substitutes that can take the place of other flowers. And remember that all flowers are beautiful, even the humblest.

*colour themes*

# White *and cream*

White has been the colour of weddings since it was popularized by Queen Victoria, who carried a posy of snowdrops and wore orange blossom in her hair at her wedding in 1840. White suggests purity and serenity, but at its most dazzling it can be harsh and unforgiving, which is why wedding dresses are often a more flattering shade of ivory or cream.

Flowers come in myriad whites, some warmed with hints of yellow or pink, others cooled with green, blue or lilac. White flowers seem to glow in the fading light of a winter afternoon or the warm dusk of a summer evening. They can look dramatic or ethereal, depending on the size and style of the bouquet. White flowers are also a perfect foil for other colours and a striking contrast to green foliage.

The simplicity of this sheaf of pristine *white arum lilies* (*Zantedeschia aethiopica*) allows the flowers to speak for themselves. The only added embellishment is a wide *pewter-coloured ribbon*, tied at the top of the stems to emphasize their flawless length. The result is a bridal bouquet that is dramatic, chic and *entirely modern*, the perfect partner for an elegant, slim-cut dress.

Almost anyone could try their hand at this arrangement, and although few flowers are needed, the finished bouquet has great presence. Although arums look *exotic*, they are available all year. There are other lilies that lend themselves to this kind of arrangement, such as longiflorum (*Lilium longiflorum*) or Oriental lilies (*Lilium auratum*), which are both *richly scented* and, like all lilies, long lasting. Delphiniums (*Delphinium*) or long-stemmed roses (*Rosa*) could be used in a similar way.

heightens the *sense of drama*. The bouquet's size balances the proportions of the bride's full-skirted dress and cathedral-length veil, producing a finished look that is highly sophisticated.

Camellias are large, *exquisitely formed flowers* and can therefore be used sparingly. Here, a single perfect flower forms the focal point of the bride's headdress. They bloom during late winter and spring, but if unavailable, white rose (*Rosa*) varieties such as Vendela, Bianca or Anne-Marie are all suitable substitutes.

*A grand wedding* demands grand flowers, but they need not be arranged in a stiff or formal way. Traditional shower bouquets are wired, but this bouquet of *pure white camellias* (*Camellia*), dainty clematis (*Clematis armandii*), camellia and clematis foliage and trailing ivy (*Hedera helix*) has been hand tied. The overall effect is spectacular but also soft and unstructured, successfully combining the romantic and the dramatic. The contrast between the waxy white camellias and dark, glossy green foliage further

This is an arrangement with *more than a hint of glamour* that would look at home partnering a dress in a *sumptuous fabric*.

The use of bare willow twigs (*Salix alba*) gives this bouquet an *unmistakably wintry feel*. Dried poppy seed heads (*Papaver*) or twisted willow (*Salix babylonica* var. *pekinensis* 'Tortuosa') would both create a similar look, adding structure and textural interest.

The effect could have been harsh, but has been softened by lightly spraying the twigs with gold paint and contrasting them with the generous open form of Bianca roses (*Rosa*) and skimmia leaves (*Skimmia*), which have also been lightly misted with gold. Paint may seem an unlikely part of a florist's tool kit but metallics in particular, when used lightly and sparingly, can create *a rich and magical effect*. Roses stand up well to being sprayed, as do arum lilies (*Zantedeschia aethiopica*). A pale gold ribbon continues the metallic theme.

This is an arrangement with more than *a hint of glamour*. It would look perfectly at home at an evening wedding, partnering a dress in a sumptuous fabric such as velvet.

This bridesmaid's bouquet is a very *grown-up and glamorous* affair. Its chic effect owes much to its simplicity, since it uses only cream Anne-Marie roses (*Rosa*) and ivy leaves (*Hedera helix*). Whites and creams are soothing, tranquil colours and are a good choice for times of the day or year when the light is poor, since they appear *almost luminous* in these conditions.

Roses remain one of the most popular flowers for weddings, not only because they're exquisitely beautiful, but also because they're easily available all year round,

good value and come in a huge variety of shades, from pristine white to a red so deep that it is almost black. Dressing up this romantic arrangement with a collar of milliner's net and a large bow of deepest purple ribbon gives it *a divinely elegant* edge. It would lend itself perfectly to a late-afternoon city wedding.

The bouquet is matched by a hair decoration fashioned from the same flowers and foliage. Another approach is to weave individual roses into the hair, or to use a single *perfect bloom* pinned to one side of the head.

*This luscious hand-tied bouquet* was designed to partner an ethereal chiffon wedding gown. The full-blown Anne-Marie roses (*Rosa*), small-leaved hebe (*Hebe*) and fronds of winter jasmine (*Jasminum nudiflorum*) combine to give the arrangement an unstructured look that is in keeping with the soft, flowing lines of the dress.

*Lengths of organza ribbon* have been fashioned into loops and swags and tied below the head of the bouquet, adding an extravagant flourish. Finishing the bouquet with this rich, shimmering bronze ribbon creates a sophisticated effect and complements the purple tinges of the hebe and the jasmine's pinky buds.

Throughout history, roses have been used as *a symbol of love*. They also have the practical advantage of being long lasting as a cut flower. Some of the new varieties look and smell much more like old-fashioned garden roses and have a beautiful, full form and delicious scent.

Finishing the bouquet with a rich, *shimmering bronze ribbon* creates a wonderfully *sophisticated* effect.

The exquisite silk ribbon that secures this generous posy of *lily of the valley* (*Convallaria majalis*) and ivy (*Hedera helix*) is just as important as the flowers. It's worth looking out for beautiful ribbon – if you find something you love, it may provide the inspiration for your floral scheme.

Although combining flowers is part of a florist's art, there's much to be said for using something as delicately beautiful as lily of the valley on its own, allowing it to take the starring role. There's an understated simplicity to this arrangement, and the bouquet is also gloriously scented.

Lily of the valley was a great favourite of the Victorians, to whom it represented *sweetness, simplicity and purity*. The plants bloom in late spring, although forced lily of the valley is available at other times of the year.

*Flower-filled baskets* brimming with blooms are a good choice for young bridesmaids, as they are easy to carry. They are also straightforward to make: the flowers are formed into bunches then arranged in the basket or inserted into a piece of florist's foam that has been cut to shape and soaked in water (line the basket with plastic to prevent any leakage). Here, *a soft and delicate* effect has been created with lily of the valley (*Convallaria majalis*) spilling over snow-white pansies (*Viola* x *wittrockiana*). Moss covers the exterior of the basket and ivy is twisted around the handle. This is *a spring arrangement,* but for a summer wedding, sweet peas (*Lathyrus odoratus*) are a good alternative.

Few things match *the freshness of green* combined with white or cream.

Few things match the freshness of green combined with white or cream. It's a timeless partnership that is soft, pretty and romantic. The colours are *calming and tranquil,* and look particularly beautiful in the clear light of spring or early summer. White and dark green can be a dramatic combination but here the use of creamy and green-tinged whites and splashes of lime create an altogether gentler effect. *This bouquet has a loose, freshly gathered feel.* It's an informal mixture of cottage-garden plants: peonies (*Paeonia*), Anne-Marie roses (*Rosa*), dill flowers (*Anethum*) and bridal wreath (*Spiraea* 'Arguta'). Peonies and bridal wreath are early summer flowerers, but at other times of year there are many other lovely white plants that could be substituted, including Canterbury bells (*Campanula medium*), marguerites (*Argyranthemum frutescens*), freesias (*Freesia*), tuberose (*Polianthes tuberosa*) or stephanotis (*Stephanotis floribunda*).

In place of the usual bouquet or posy, the little bridesmaid carries a hoop of Anne-Marie roses, lisianthus (*Eustoma*), bridal wreath, variegated ivy (*Hedera helix*) and euonymus (*Euonymus*), finished with a loose *flourish of white ribbon.*

# Yellow

This primary colour brings with it a splash of sunshine. It's light and cheerful, and because of these qualities it seems to glows in poor light. There are cool and warm shades of yellow, and the two don't mix well. Clear, acid yellows have a distinct greenish tinge, while rich golden yellows contain warm red undertones. Sharp lemon yellows can be overpowering and may need toning down with white, cream, green or soft blue.

Yellow is a predominant colour in the spring garden, particularly in its more acid forms, and is at home in this season's clear and gentle light. Summer's stronger light suits brighter shades of this colour, while the mellow days of autumn are the perfect setting for orangey yellows.

This simple bunch of flowers is *refreshingly informal,* the very opposite of the traditional, structured bridal bouquet.

I wanted it to look as if it had been freshly gathered from *a summer meadow,* so have used yellow pot marigolds (*Calendula officinalis*), Scarborough lilies (*Cyrtanthus elatus*), fritillaries (*Fritillaria michailovskyi*) and daisy-like feverfew (*Tanacetum parthenium*). Good substitutes would be African daisies (*Gerbera*), marguerites (*Argyranthemum frutescens*), globe flowers (*Trollius*) and cow parsley (*Anthriscus sylvestris*). The colour scheme of *rich gold* and lemon yellow with white and green evokes sunny days and country lanes. The loose construction of the bouquet gives it a beguiling feel of openness and spontaneity.

Inspiration for flower arrangements can come from anywhere. The pretty braid that cinches the stem of this *neat little posy* was the starting point for its fresh, spring-like yellow and green colour scheme. It uses two *deliciously scented* spring plants: narcissi (*Narcissus poeticus* 'Cheerfulness') and mimosa (*Acacia dealbata*). Although some narcissi come in rather brash shades of yellow, this variety has a rich and creamy hue. Their *delicate, starry little blooms* complement the mimosa's tiny pompom-like flowers and fine leaves, creating an overall effect that is exquisitely pretty, feminine and understated.

The flower-patterned braid has been wound into two fine bands around the stems and carefully secured with *pearl-headed pins*. The arrangement's slender proportions give it an elegant silhouette and the long stems also make it easy to carry.

This cheerful bunch encapsulates all *the promise of spring*. Yellow flowers at this time of year tend to have more green than red in their colouring, and although these cool acid yellows can look harsh in bright sunlight, in the weaker light of spring they are fresh and appealing.

Daffodils are one of *the stars of the spring season*. Here, two varieties of daffodil (*Narcissus* 'Carlton' and 'Ice Follies') have been combined with narcissi (*N. poeticus* 'Cheerfulness'), yellow and golden ranunculus (*Ranunculus asiaticus*), lime-green guelder rose (*Viburnum opulus*), white spring snowflakes (*Leucojum vernum*) and grey-green senecio (*Senecio*). The bouquet is *charmingly rustic* and, when finished off with a length of yellow gingham ribbon, looks as pretty as a picture.

*Floral circlets* are alway popular, especially for little bridesmaids. This one is distinctly Pre-Raphaelite in feel, a crown of yellow and white spring blooms. Like the bouquet it complements, it uses daffodils (*Narcissi* 'Carlton' and 'Ice Follies'), narcissi (*N.* 'Cheerfulness') ranunculus (*Ranunculus asiaticus*), spring snowflakes (*Leucojum vernum*), guelder rose (*Viburnum opulus*) and senecio (*Senecio*).

Headdresses are one of the more labour-intensive and expensive arrangements in a florist's repertoire, since all the flowers have to be wired before use. Keep them refrigerated for as long as possible before the ceremony and, if they're being worn by *young bridesmaids*, put them on at the very last minute so that they don't get too squashed or pulled about!

Allowing *roses* to take centre stage in this way permits their *full beauty* to be appreciated.

Simplicity and chic often go hand in hand. This domed bouquet of Illios roses (*Rosa*) is both *elegant and dramatic* in its use of a single type and colour of flower. Allowing the roses to take centre stage in this way permits their intricate and delicate form and their glorious golden hue, which fades to a paler shade on the outer petals, to be appreciated. I finished the bouquet with *ruched cream silk* pinned with pearl-headed pins, and greeny-bronze ribbon to give it a *dressed-up look*.

The end result is an arrangement that is decidedly ladylike and grown-up, perfect for a traditional wedding in a grand setting. Roses are available all year, making this bouquet a versatile design that could be used as a vehicle for many other colours.

*Orange*

Orange runs a close second behind red for intensity and warmth, while the presence of yellow in its make-up makes it a cheerful and uplifting colour. At its zingy brightest, it can be challenging to work with, although if successful the results can be spectacular. At the edges of the orange spectrum lie harmonizing tones such as pale apricot, peach, amber and buff – softer, gentler colours that are easier to handle.

Orange is improved by the increasingly mellow light of late summer and autumn, when the colour comes into its own in the garden and seems to glow. Orange can be combined very successfully with other warm colours – yellows, golds, terracottas or brick reds – for a spirited, sizzling look, or cooled down with blues, greens or purples.

Tulips (*Tulipa*) are one of my *favourite flowers*. They are available for much of the year; are good value for money; have an elegant shape and silky petals; and come in *a rainbow of sumptuous colours*. Used *en masse*, as here, their handsome looks are seen to good advantage. Peachy orange tulips streaked with yellow are partnered with a dusky purple variety for a daring but surprisingly effective combination, producing an *opulent and splendid* result. The flowers have been tightly packed into a large, round bouquet, the shape of the arrangement emphasized by the outer ring of *purple blooms*. I have used silver wire to embellish the tulips in two different ways. For one bouquet (*this page*), it simply binds the stems; for the other (*see previous page*), I have looped it loosely across and around the head of the bouquet to create an effect that is reminiscent of a piece of modern sculpture.

The *Iceland poppy* (*Papaver croceum*) is one of the only members of its family that can be used successfully as a cut flower – the secret to making the blooms last is to singe the bottom of the stems.

The plants have fine, silky petals, feathery centres and intriguingly hairy stems, and come in *clear, vivid colours* ranging from creams and yellows to oranges, reds and pinks. They're jolly and exuberant flowers that look pretty gathered into a simple, informal bunch and finished with a lime-green ribbon *edged in rosy pink*. Iceland poppies are available on and off throughout the year, but African daisies (*Gerbera*), which come in a similar range of colours, are a possible substitute.

Iceland poppies have fine, *silky petals*, feathery centres and intriguingly hairy stems, and come in *clear, vivid colours*.

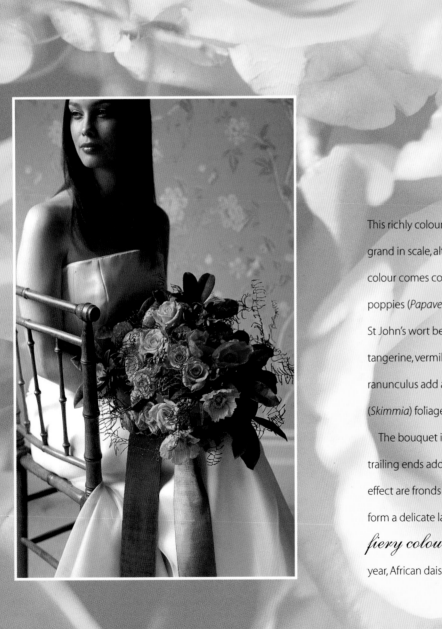

This richly coloured bouquet is *sophisticated in mood* and grand in scale, although it's loose and unstructured in shape. The intense colour comes courtesy of vibrant Naranja and Decca roses (*Rosa*), Iceland poppies (*Papaver croceum*), ranunculus (*Ranunculus asiaticus*) and St John's wort berries (*Hypericum*) in shades of *burnt orange*, tangerine, vermilion and golden yellow. The lime-green centres of the ranunculus add a dash of sharp contrast, while hebe (*Hebe*) and skimmia (*Skimmia*) foliage create a backdrop of dark, moody greens.

The bouquet is tied with a gleaming copper-brown ribbon whose long, trailing ends add *drama and glamour*. Lightening the whole effect are fronds of feathery coral fern (*Thelypteris patens* var. *lepids*), which form a delicate lattice over the flowers and foliage. A bouquet with these *fiery colours* is suited to late summer or autumn. At other times of year, African daisies (*Gerbera*) and dahlias (*Dahlia*) are possible alternatives.

Sandersonia (*Sandersonia*) is such an *elegant* and distinctive plant that it almost demands to be used on its own. Its little Chinese lantern-like flowers are palest apricot and are partnered by *slender grass-green leaves*. The stems need little conditioning and are a good choice if you want make your own bouquet.

Here, I've gathered a sheaf of sandersonia into a loose bunch that emphasizes the plant's *dainty delicacy*. Bronze organza ribbon has been tied into soft loops, with the ends left long to balance the length of the bouquet. Such a simple arrangement looks at its best with an unfussy dress. Here, it complements a strapless gown with a filmy organza skirt.

Sandersonia's little *Chinese lantern-like* flowers are palest apricot and partnered by *slender grass-green leaves.*

*Sweet peas* (*Lathyrus odoratus*) are a traditional favourite. It's not hard to see why: they have delicate ruffled petals, come in a broad range of beautiful colours and have a delightful scent. Old-fashioned varieties have the sweetest fragrance, but their flowers are smaller than the modern varieties and come in a narrower range of colours.

Modern sweet peas come in whites, pinks, blues, purples and reds, but more unusual shades can sometimes be found. *This unashamedly pretty bouquet* is made up of a mouthwatering array of the flowers in shades of cream, pale yellow, apricot and tangerine. They have been loosely gathered into a bunch with a froth of lady's mantle (*Alchemilla mollis*), and bound with a striped ribbon.

# Red

Passionate and intense, red is the most powerful of the primary colours. A symbol of love and fire, this vibrant colour can be overpowering in excess and needs to be used with caution. Red's natural opposite on the colour wheel is green, which helps to tone it down, as do white and cream.

Warm, orangey reds such as scarlet are the boldest and brightest members of the red family and are a good match for the strong, bleaching light of midsummer. Cooler, blue-based reds such as crimson are less vivid and exhilarating but look strong and rich in the cool, thin light of winter.

Roses (*Rosa*) are available in myriad *luscious reds* all year round, and in this glamorous formal bouquet I've used three of my favourites: Lipstick, Grand Prix and Tamango, a spray rose. To break up the reds, dark green photinia (*Photinia*) foliage and flowers have been added. A generous ruff of sheer crimson fabric (the type used by milliners) and stems of *trailing ivy* (*Hedera helix*) finish the bouquet beautifully.

This is a dramatic arrangement in terms of both shape and colour. It's not the ideal partner for a very full or flouncy dress, demanding instead something simple and structured. A neat, rounded bridesmaid's bouquet fashioned from Lipstick and Grand Prix roses with skimmia (*Skimmia*) leaves and flowers and deep red ribbon partners the bride's bouquet.

The rose is the *classic wedding flower*, but there are a multitude of other wonderful red options, including bold African daisies (*Gerbera*), carnations (*Dianthus*) and exotic glory lilies (*Gloriosa superba*).

Red moves towards the purple end of the spectrum in this *elegant bouquet*, which combines peonies (*Paeonia*), Lipstick roses (*Rosa*), cockscomb (*Celosia*), love-lies-bleeding (*Amaranthus caudatus*) and peony leaves. The variety of red tones brings depth and complexity of colour to the bouquet. As well as the ruby-red peonies, there is *soft pink* on the outside of the rose petals, hints of cerise in the chenille-like ruffles of the cockscomb, and the burgundy of the love-lies-bleeding. There's also *richness of texture*, from the feathery centres of the peonies to the velvety cockscomb. The matching hair decoration makes use of the flowers' sculptural forms.

This dramatic bridal bouquet strikes a wintry note. *Ruby-red* Grand Prix roses (*Rosa*) are teamed with amaryllis (*Hippeastrum*), winter jasmine (*Jasminum nudiflorum*), pine (*Pinus*) foliage, camellia (*Camellia*) leaves, ivy (*Hedera helix*) and silvery cones.

The light in midwinter is cold and hard, but forest greens and cool reds work well in this unforgiving environment. The rich red of the roses and amaryllis is delicately echoed by the *pinky-red buds* of the winter jasmine, while touches of cream on the variegated ivy leaves give a lift to the other, more sombre foliage. The silver accents are a wonderfully wintry foil for the

other colours. There is plenty of textural interest here, too, in the feathery jasmine, bristly pine foliage and velvety rose petals.

The shape of the bouquet adds to its romantic effect. Because it is tied rather than wired, the arrangement has an artless, random look, which is emphasized by the *tumbling stems of trailing ivy*.

For brides with adventurous tastes, *a visit to the tropics* might appeal. This spectacular arrangement of heliconias (*Heliconia*), ginger lilies (*Alpinia*) and palm leaves (*Phoenix*) is about as far removed from a traditional bouquet as it's possible to get, and although the blooms exude exoticism, they're actually available all year round.

Heliconias and ginger lilies are expensive, but they're so dramatic that they can be used sparingly and still produce a head-turning effect. Here, however, I've used them generously for *maximum drama*. The stems have been kept long to create a strong, upright shape, while the palm leaves are fanned outwards to provide balance.

The colour scheme is hot and exuberant, with pinky-red and spicy orange blooms cooled by the softer, coral-pink ones and the lush green leaves. All these colours are picked out by the *rainbow-coloured ribbon* used to tie the arrangement.

*Pink*

This most feminine of colours is one of the most popular for weddings, particularly in its softest, most blushing shades. The pink spectrum ranges all the way from cool, pastel pinks with blue undertones that merge into lilac, to warm, yellow-tinged pinks that edge towards salmon, peach and coral. In general, however, a combination of shades from the two ends of the pink spectrum won't add up to a pleasing partnership.

All pinks are flattering and romantic, but different shades produce different effects. Pale pinks are calming and restful, while deeper pink shades such as cerise, fuchsia and magenta are associated with all things passionate and dramatic. Green is pink's natural contrast. Cool pinks look wonderful when combined with silver, purple and blue. Pink can even be paired with red to achieve a bold and vivid, but very stylish, effect.

*Warm, pretty and feminine*, pale pink is the most popular wedding colour after white and cream. This bridal bouquet, with its pastel pink theme, is classic in shape and composition – perfect for a grand or traditional wedding. However, since it is a tied bouquet, it still manages to retain a certain artless and natural quality.

Roses (*Rosa*) are *eternally romantic*. Here, creamy pink Candy Bianca complements white and pink lilies (*Lilium*). The lilies' stamens have been removed, because the pollen stains anything it touches. There's also pink-budded jasmine (*Jasminum*), photinia (*Photinia*) foliage and flowers, kangaroo paw (*Anigozanthos*) and ceanothus (*Ceanothus*) leaves, and a flourish of bronze-green ribbon. Touches of stronger colour – the dark and

This bridal bouquet, with its *pastel pink* theme, is *classic in shape* and composition.

lime-green foliage, and the deep pink of the jasmine – prevent the pale pink from becoming insipid. To complete the ensemble, the bride wears a single, perfect *Candy Bianca rose* in her hair.

The bridesmaid's bouquet uses many of the same plants, with a few additions, such as Nostalgia roses. It's a generous, hand-tied bunch, the stems left long and tied with the same *bronze-green ribbon*. The blush-pink markings on the outside of the Nostalgia roses and the russet leaves of the photinia make the colour scheme slightly more emphatic.

Red and pink may sound like an unlikely wedding combination, but the colours are variations on the same theme. It's hard to make them work together, but this bouquet shows how stunning they can look when handled skilfully. *Vibrant colours abound* – there are shocking-pink sweet peas (*Lathyrus odoratus*), scarlet and gold glory lilies (*Gloriosa superba*), and a trio of roses (*Rosa*): soft pink Nostalgia, darkest red *Black Beauty* and ruby-red Tamango, along with skimmia (*Skimmia*) foliage. The colours are strong but the overall effect is rich rather than riotous. The key to the success of the scheme is that the hot colours are tempered by darker or lighter ones. These balance the bouquet, while the ribbon brings everything together by picking out colours present in the flowers.

The key to the success of this scheme is that the *hot colours* are tempered by lighter or darker ones.

This posy of white poppy anemones (*Anemone coronaria* De Caen) tinged with *softest pink* proves that pale can be interesting. The black centres of the flowers contrast beautifully with the flimsy petals, whose colouring gives them an almost iridescent quality. The finishing touch is a collar of silver organza and a cranberry satin bow.

The success of this sort of *deceptively simple* bouquet depends on a generous use of flowers to create *a luxuriant effect,* so don't be tempted to skimp. Although naturally spring-flowering plants, anemones are now commercially available in the winter and autumn, too.

This bridesmaid's posy of cerise Singapore orchids (*Dendrobium*) is small but perfectly formed. Despite their *exotic looks,* these flowers are available all year and are not too expensive. The orchids' waxy petals are exquisitely shaped and their deep hue is enhanced by delicate white shading at the bottom of the petals.

Flowers as beautiful as this should be allowed to take centre stage, so they have simply been tied into a pretty little bunch with the stems bound in ruched satin trimming to add a little *extra glamour.*

Glamorous yet *romantic*, this bouquet would look wonderful at a *sophisticated evening* reception.

Flowers can and should be fun. This bouquet goes all out for colour and glamour, with *a touch of sparkle* thrown in for good measure. A ravishing array of roses (*Rosa*) – Martinique, Grand Prix, Ravel and Jacaranda – in burgundy, ruby red and deep pink have been arranged into a tightly packed dome. Spray-on glue has been spritzed over the flowers, followed by *a sprinkling of red and purple glitter*. Dark red velvet and wide pink ribbon finish the arrangement. This is a bouquet for a bride with a sense of fun. It's glamorous yet romantic, and would look wonderful at a sophisticated evening reception.

What could be more bridal and romantic than pink roses (*Rosa*)? Here, they're an *old-fashioned garden rose* with a fabulous open form in a strong, clear pink. They're also subtly shaded, with petals that are pale on the outside and more *deeply coloured* within. I've paired them with lilac-pink hydrangea (*Hydrangea*), some of whose unopened buds are greenish white. The stems have been left long, giving the bouquet an elegant shape.

The flowers make an effective pairing, not only because the colours harmonize well but also because the blooms have such different forms, making for richness of texture. What they have in common, however, is *gracefulness and delicacy*, the hydrangea with its tiny, frothy heads, the roses with their fine, curved petals. The bouquet has an air of informality and *uncontrived natural beauty*.

*Purple*

A mixture of red and blue, purple has two moods depending on which primary predominates: warm when it's red, cool if it's blue. Purple ranges from shades so moody they are almost black all the way through to wistful mauves and palest tints of lilac.

Different shades of purple work well together. Deep purples are regal and dramatic and can be successfully mixed with dark red, blue or pink for a rich, jewel-like effect. Lighter variations combine the restfulness of soft blue with the prettiness of pale pink and look good with both of those colours.

Deep coloured and soft textured, this dramatic bouquet is as *lustrous as velvet*. It uses poppy anemones (*Anemone coronaria* De Caen), ranunculus (*Ranunculus asiaticus*) and sweet peas (*Lathyrus odoratus*) in a palette of purples from lilac to violet, and is tied with purple ribbon.

The bouquet makes *a strong statement*, and not only in terms of colour. The size and the long stems add to its *stately presence*. The matching headdress of sweet peas finishes the ensemble beautifully. A striking effect has been created by graduating the flowers from pale to dark – an idea that can be reproduced with any flower that comes in a wide range of colours, such as roses (*Rosa*).

Snakeshead fritillaries (*Fritillaria meleagris*) are such *beautiful and unusual* flowers that they can be arranged in the simplest and most understated of ways. Here, I've gathered them into a loose sheaf along with their leaves, an arrangement that anyone could tackle.

*Organza ribbon*, shaded from green to softest purple pink and teamed with a narrow green ribbon, echoes the flowers' subtle colouring and fragility. The fritillaries' chequered maroon bells have an understated appeal, but their delicacy makes them undeniably romantic.

The *sweet pea* is a cottage-garden favourite available in a *huge range of colours*.

Few flowers are as *unashamedly pretty* or gloriously scented as the sweet pea (*Lathyrus odoratus*), a cottage-garden favourite that is available in a huge range of colours. In shades of lilac and violet, they are so ravishing that the only way to use them is on their own.

The flowers have been gathered into a teardrop-shaped bunch and the stems bound with purple ribbon, which is held in place with *tiny pearl-headed pins*. The effect is breathtaking, not just because of the beautiful, luscious colours but also because of the silky texture and delicate shape of the *ruffled petals*. Scent adds another sensory dimension.

Sweet peas are not available all year; they're found in flower markets from late spring until early to midsummer, though they can be sown in the garden in late spring, extending their flowering period through the summer.

Some colour schemes are made for the day, others for the evening. This is one of the latter, *a sophisticated mixture* of sultry burgundy, royal purple and shocking pink, highlighted with pink-tinged white. With its dressy bow and ribbon-bound stem, the bouquet suggests glamour and sophistication, *dancing and champagne*.

The bouquet is tightly packed with flowers, a mixture of ranunculus (*Ranunculus asiaticus*), Black Beauty roses (*Rosa*) and sweet peas (*Lathyrus odoratus*). No foliage has been used, so the *rich colours* of the blooms are unadulterated. Sweet peas are available from late spring to midsummer, and ranunculuses from midwinter through to spring and again in autumn. Possible substitutes are lisianthus (*Eustoma*), which are available all year round in similar colours.

The *soft, muted* colours are reminiscent of the limpid light of *long summer* evenings.

This summer bouquet captures purple in a gentle mood, fading to *lilac and pinky mauve*. The palette is soft and subdued, but given extra depth by accents of deeper colour. I've used ice-cream pink peonies (*Paeonia*), Blue Curiosa roses (*Rosa*), blue flag irises (*Iris versicolor*), and clematis (*Clematis*), hebe (*Hebe*) and skimmia (*Skimmia*) foliage. Two ribbons tie the bouquet, one purply blue, picking out the irises' darker tones; and one cerise, complementing the peonies. This is *a romantic arrangement*, its soft and muted colours reminiscent of the limpid light of long summer evenings.

Peonies are treasured by gardeners and florists alike because of their *outstanding beauty* and their short flowering period in early summer. If they're not available, full-blown pale pink roses (such as Candy Bianca) could take their place. Flag irises are in flower from early- to midsummer but could be replaced with scabious (*Scabiosa*) in high summer.

and other materials are wired before being stuck into a ball of florist's foam, then a ribbon handle is attached. Ranunculus and pansies are available in winter and spring, while cineraria and African violets are pot plants and can be found in garden centres for much of the year.

Other *small-headed flowers* could be used to create a similar effect. Try covering a ball with small-headed roses, snipped off just below the flower head. Their stems are strong enough not to need wiring.

This butterfly ball is *frivolous and fun*, but it's also romantic and vibrant, an outrageously pretty composition of violet and purple, sugary pink and turquoise. The colours are clear and fresh, the darker shades setting off the lighter ones. For a touch of fantasy, I've used beaded tassels, feathers and *feather butterflies* alongside ranunculus (*Ranunculus asiaticus*), pansies (*Viola* x *wittrockiana*), cineraria (*Cineraria*) and African violets (*Saintpaulia*).

Floral balls like this are complicated to make, and must be kept cold until the last minute. The flowers

Rich purple and soft blue is a lush and dreamy combination, as demonstrated here with a posy of sumptuous gloxinias (*Sinningia speciosa*) and *deliciously scented* hyacinths (*Hyacinthus*), surrounded by variegated hosta (*Hosta*) leaves.

This is a sophisticated little arrangement with just a hint of the exotic. Gloxinias are greenhouse pot plants and are usually found in garden centres rather than flower markets. Their bell-like flowers have beautifully silky petals, and their delicacy of texture is set off by the *sparkling organza* ribbon used to tie the posy. Hyacinths are readily available throughout the late winter and spring months, and aren't expensive. If Gloxinias are unavailable, sweet peas (*Lathyrus odoratus*) or poppy anemones (*Anemone coronaria* De Caen) in a similar colour could be used.

Pansies (*Viola* x *wittrockiana*) and *forget-me-nots* (*Myosotis*) are old-fashioned spring favourites, here combined in a charming bouquet in the Victorian style, the flowers arranged in concentric circles.

*The tiny, starry heads* of the forget-me-nots and the velvety, open pansies are a study in contrast, with the soft sky blue of one setting off the sumptuous purple of the other. A regal purple ribbon collar, fashioned into 'petals', highlights the bouquet's neat shape. The finishing touch to this bridesmaid's outfit is a delicate *circlet of pansies*. It's details such as this that help to make arrangements special and distinctive.

*Blue*

Dreamy, serene and peaceful, blue is less common in the flower kingdom than other colours. The coolest primary, blue blends into purple to produce shades of lavender and ranges through a series of true blue shades to merge with green and become turquoise.

Bright, clear blues lift the spirits, like the sight of a cloudless azure sky, and look more intense in hot sunshine. Misty blues tinged with grey or purple are more tranquil and atmospheric, and some pale blues look luminescent at twilight. White, cream, silver, cool pink and purple blend harmoniously with blue, while yellow makes it look richer and stronger.

Thanks to the traditional rhyme
*'Something old,*
*Something new'*
blue is a popular wedding colour.

True blues are relatively uncommon in the plant world, but this mophead hydrangea (*Hydrangea macrophylla*) is the *pure blue* of a cloudless summer sky. Blue is a popular wedding colour not only because of its place in the traditional rhyme 'Something old, Something new' but also because it flatters most skin and hair colours.

For these two little bridesmaids, I wired hydrangea florets into thick circlets with a base of variegated ivy leaves (*Hedera helix*) and pompom-like floral balls with sky- and sapphire-blue ribbon handles and streamers. The bride carries a long, loose bouquet with hydrangeas at its base, from which a cascade of delphiniums (*Delphinium*), sea holly (*Eryngium*) and variegated ivy tumble to create *a lusciously abundant effect*.

Forced hydrangea can be found in flower markets in early summer but its proper flowering season is from midsummer to early autumn, when it can be found in the garden. For full depth of colour, the flower heads must be completely open but they look very attractive both before the colour develops and after its peak as it begins to fade and becomes tinged with other shades. Here, they are at their most intense, their piercing colour and soft, open form producing *a dreamy, romantic look*.

The long stems and compact head of this *dainty posy* give it a pretty *lollipop* shape, making it light and easy to hold.

There's *a beautiful simplicity* about this neat little posy. Grape hyacinths (*Muscari*) and annual cornflowers (*Centaurea cyanus*) have been tightly bunched together and tied with narrow navy ribbon. The tiny bells of the grape hyacinths and the cornflowers' feathery petals provide a pleasing *textural contrast* and their subtly different shades – the grape hyacinths fading to a gentle sky blue, the cornflowers with richer purple undertones – set each other off perfectly. The long stems and compact head of the posy give it a pretty lollipop shape, making it light and easy to hold.

Grape hyacinths flower from spring to early summer and cornflowers can be found from early until late summer. Both are widely available and inexpensive. Other blue flowers that could be used in a similar way for *a summery posy* include love-in-a-mist (*Nigella*), scabious (*Scabiosa*) and gentians (*Gentiana*).

*Flower-filled baskets* are a pretty alternative to posies for little bridesmaids. This arrangement is a variation on the theme, using a miniature galvanized-metal bucket with a handle made from pussy willow (*Salix caprea* 'Kilmarnock'). I've filled the bucket with an array of spring bulbs: grape hyacinths (*Muscari*), bluebells (*Hyacinthoides non-scripta*) and white Spanish bluebells (*Hyacinthoides hispanica*). Blue and white is a pretty combination that always looks *simple and fresh*, and as an added bonus the flowers are sweetly scented. Good alternatives include forget-me-nots (*Myosotis*), spring snowflakes (*Leucojum vernum*), hyacinths (*Hyacinthus*) and dwarf irises (*Iris reticulata*).

This is a simple and inexpensive idea that produces *a glorious effect*. I've filled an old wicker basket with stem upon stem of bluebells (*Hyacinthoides non-scripta*) and decorated it with a rich cobalt ribbon.

These *humble but gorgeous* flowers are one of the great joys of spring, when they form blue carpets in gardens and woods. As well as being richly coloured, they are also deliciously scented. Bluebells can be bought inexpensively from flower markets but, even better, are to be found in some gardens, so this arrangement could be put together for nothing. Remember, however, that bluebells are protected and should never be picked from the wild.

The basket could be filled with loose stems but I think it's a nice idea to tie the flowers into bunches and give them to guests at the reception. For *a summer wedding*, cornflowers (*Centaurea cyanus*) would be a good alternative.

Enveloping the bouquet in *a cloud of cream tulle* creates a romantic soft-focus effect.

Dyed roses (*Rosa*), which have absorbed coloured water through their stems, can be obtained from flower markets, often in very *vivid hues*. Electric-blue roses look bold and dramatic and will appeal to brides with adventurous tastes. They're *undeniably eye-catching* and, unlikely though it may seem, can be used to produce a bouquet that is still unmistakably bridal.

Partnering the roses with grey-green senecio (*Senecio*) foliage and enveloping the bouquet in a cloud of cream tulle creates a romantic *soft-focus effect*, toning down the colour of the flowers. Using tulle in this way is a novel idea that can be applied to other arrangements. It is best used over richly coloured flowers and those with a strong form that will still be visible through the diaphanous fabric.

# Green

Green is the predominant colour of the natural landscape and there are shades to complement every other colour. It embraces myriad variations, from silvery grey greens to acidic lime greens, through bright apple greens and on to the muted greens of a pine forest. There are many plants with interestingly variegated foliage and even some with green flowers.

Green is cool, tranquil and fresh, though at its strongest it can look tropical and jungly. Cream, white, blue and yellow combine harmoniously with soft green, while more striking effects can be created by mixing stronger greens with contrasting red, pink or purple.

These posies and bouquet are *a gentle harmony* of lime, apple and yellowy greens, perfect for a spring wedding. The bride's bouquet uses a mixture of cottage-garden and exotic flowers: hellebores (*Helleborus*), Singapore orchids (*Dendrobium*), proteas (*Protea*), guelder rose (*Viburnum opulus*) and laurustinus (*Viburnum tinus*). The result is *a luxuriant arrangement* with lots of variation in shape and texture.

Good alternatives would be bells of Ireland (*Moluccella laevis*), green chrysanthemums (*Chrysanthemum* 'Kermit') or lisianthus (*Eustoma*). The bridesmaids' posies differ slightly. One has *a ruff of ivy leaves* (*Hedera helix*) peeping out from behind the flowers, while the other has been arranged in precise concentric circles in the Victorian style.

This bouquet of cymbidium orchids (*Cymbidium*), kangaroo paw (*Anigozanthos*), galax leaves (*Galax*) and lady's mantle (*Alchemilla mollis*) is *a subtle marriage* of exotic plants and a cottage-garden favourite. Textural interest is offered by the glossy galax, the waxy orchid petals and the *frothy cloud* of lady's mantle. Cymbidium orchids and kangaroo paw are available all year round. Lady's mantle is a summer plant, but a similar effect could be achieved by using euphorbia (*Euphorbia*), which is available all year.

When using *green on green*, it's important to have variation in *shape and texture* as well as colour.

Elizabethan brides carried *posies of herbs* in the belief that they provided protection against evil spirits. Herbs can be used in mixed bouquets but are also attractive enough to be used on their own. They smell wonderful, particularly on a sunny day, when the warmth helps to release their aromatic oils. Many herbs also have the bonus of pretty flowers in summer.

Here, I've gathered together rosemary (*Rosmarinus officinalis*), golden marjoram (*Origanum vulgare* 'Aureum'), thyme (*Thymus vulgaris*), sage (*Salvia officinalis*) and tarragon (*Artemisia dracunculus*) and decorated them with *ribbon streamers* in shades of soft green. When using green on green it's always important to include plenty of variation in shape and texture as well as colour. Here, there are round, oval and needle-like leaves. Those of the marjoram have a dull gleam, while the *silvery sage foliage* is soft and downy.

Blue and green are *harmonious partners*, and in these gentle tones make for a *restful colour scheme*.

The *Victorian method* of making bridal posies, whereby the flowers are wired and arranged into neat concentric circles, creates a prim yet pretty effect. Here, lime greens and soft blues produce a demure look, reflecting the fresh colours of spring. Glossy green galax (*Galax*) leaves form an outer collar, followed by tightly packed layers of guelder rose (*Viburnum opulus*), green lisianthus (*Eustoma*) and *fragrant blue hyacinths* (*Hyacinthus*).

Blue and green are harmonious partners, and in these gentle tones make for a restful colour scheme. Blue cornflowers (*Centaurea*) or hydrangea (*Hydrangea*) florets, which are tinged green when young, would be good substitutes for the hyacinths, and lady's mantle (*Alchemilla mollis*) or green Singapore orchids (*Dendrobium*) for the guelder rose.

These two floral balls show how *striking and romantic* green on green can look. The first (in the foreground) uses cymbidium orchids (*Cymbidium*) and skimmia (*Skimmia*) leaves, whose slender, pointed shape echoes the flowers' *elegant petals*. Both plants are available all year, making this a useful combination for winter, when the range of flowers available can be limited. The second ball combines cymbidium orchids with frothy, summer-flowering lady's mantle (*Alchemilla mollis*), which produces a looser, more informal effect.

Bold reds, pinks and purples are good foils for strong greens. Here, the delicate burgundy markings on the orchids are complemented by a rich purple ribbon with a cerise-pink edge, which injects *vibrancy* into the scheme. Floral balls are time-consuming to make, as the flowers must be wired before being inserted into a ball of florist's foam. However, they're light and easy to carry, making them a good option for young bridesmaids.

*colour combinations*

# Romantic

Cool, harmonious colours in ice-cream shades – gentle blues, soft lilacs, baby pinks and mint greens – are wonderful if you want to create a dreamy, soft-focus effect with your bridal flowers.

Pastels are undeniably feminine and pretty but don't forget that deeper purples and vibrant reds can look every bit as romantic, particularly when mixed with lots of white or cream, which add freshness and light.

Texture is also important. For a romantic effect, choose fragile, intricate blooms – opulent, full-blown roses, foamy heads of lilac, silky sweet peas – and highlight them with foliage in muted shades of green.

This bouquet is *lavish and luscious*, a combination of sweet peas (*Lathyrus odoratus*) and poppy anemones (*Anemone coronaria* De Caen). The sweet peas range from cream to rich yellow to soft apricot and are punctuated by the bold scarlet anemones, whose large black centres give them further emphasis. The arrangement is finished with pale yellow net and a bow of *sunflower yellow* ribbon. These hot colours complement each other wonderfully well, but be warned – with such emphatic shades it's easy to overdo it. Here, though, the sweet peas are sufficiently gentle in tone that they don't battle with the vivid red of the anemones. The overall effect is *bright but not garish*.

These *candy colours* look most at home in the strong light of summer, a time of year when *bold and bright* flowers come into their own.

Roses remain the *most popular* of all flowers for weddings. This pretty idea for little bridesmaids is a new way to arrange them. Small woven baskets have been filled with *patio roses* in sugar pink, dark pink and golden yellow and then decorated with mint-green and pale pink ribbons. It's a simple but effective idea that could easily be done at home.

Pink and yellow might seem an unexpected combination, but here it works beautifully because the pinks are warm and the yellow is tinged with red. These *candy colours* look most at home in the strong light of summer, a time of year when bold and bright flowers come into their own.

The familiar white daisies of childhood have given rise over the decades to other, cultivated varieties. These *daisies* (*Bellis*), with their dainty *pompom-like flowers*, are available as bedding plants from garden centres and have a long flowering period, from March until July.

Here, they've been used with clusters of vivid blue forget-me-nots (*Myosotis*) and ivy leaves (*Hedera helix*) to make adorable posies for two little bridesmaids. The colour scheme is unashamedly pretty, combining snow white, candy pink and sky blue.

If young bridesmaids are to carry flowers, it's important to keep the arrangements in scale so that they don't look overwhelming. These *dreamy little posies* are just right: they're neat and light to carry and use appropriately small flowers. Matching circlets have been fashioned from pink daisies and ivy leaves. Worn with simple white dresses, the overall effect is *utterly enchanting*.

With its *summery colour scheme* of clear pink, lilac and soft lime green, this bridesmaids' garland is irresistibly romantic and pretty. The only drawback is that, as with any wired arrangement, a garland is a time-consuming project for a florist, so will be more expensive than tied bouquets.

The flowers used here and for the bride's bouquet are *cottage-garden favourites*, full of old-fashioned charm. The garland combines pink garden roses (*Rosa*), lacecap hydrangea (*Hydrangea macrophylla*), lilac (*Syringa*), guelder rose (*Viburnum opulus*) and viburnum flowers (*Viburnum davidii*). It's a lavish arrangement with a relaxed pastoral feel.

The bride's bouquet is full and unstructured, a mass of *sugar pink and fresh green*. Columbines (*Aquilegia*), opulent garden roses and parrot tulips (*Tulipa*) in ice-cream shades sit alongside the pompom heads of lime-green guelder rose.

I love these *floral maypoles* – they're such a pretty and unusual idea for little bridesmaids and they aren't difficult to make. Two short broomsticks have been wrapped in contrasting pastel shades of ribbon, then small posies have been bound to the tops of the poles with wire. Ribbon streamers disguise the joins and add a festive finishing touch.

To continue the theme of *a countryside celebration*, cottage-garden flowers have also been used for the posies: pansies (*Viola* x *wittrockiana*), daisies (*Bellis*) and forget-me-nots (*Myosotis*) for one, and pansies, daisies and columbines (*Aquilegia*) for the other. The purple pansies add depth to the soft sugared-almond shades of baby pink, palest blue and mint green. These are all spring to early summer flowers and could be replaced later in the summer by other garden plants such as scabious (*Scabiosa*), pinks (*Dianthus*) or cornflowers (*Centaurea cyanus*).

The bride carries a sheaf of *apple blossom* (*Malus*), tied with a rich purple ribbon that picks up the colour of the pansies. Alternatives for later in the summer include white and pale pink delphiniums (*Delphinium*) or phlox (*Phlox*).

Lilac (*Syringa*) heralds *the arrival of summer,* producing plumes of sweetly scented flowers in whites and pinks as well as lilac itself. Here, *a two-tone effect* has been created by bunching stems into a large, casual bouquet, tied with a wide purple ribbon and a narrower white one. Alternatively, the colours could be mingled or used on their own. Arranged *en masse* like this, lilac works well without any additional foliage, allowing the delicate blooms to be seen to full advantage. The effect is romantic, natural and uncontrived, and the colours soft and flattering.

The diminutive *circlet of lilac* could be carried by a bridesmaid in place of a posy. Cream and lilac blooms have been intermingled, and little skimmia (*Skimmia*) leaves added for contrast of form and colour. Two tones of rich purple satin ribbon add a final flourish.

The tiny *nodding bells* of lily of the valley (*Convallaria majalis*) have a charmingly old-fashioned air.

It's a traditional wedding flower that is valued for its scent and delicate form. Lily of the valley was a

favourite of the Victorians, who associated it with sweetness, *delicate simplicity* and purity. Here,

it has been tied into a posy with purple violets (*Viola cornuta*), another old-fashioned favourite.

To give the flowers *a modern touch*, I've wrapped them in a spiral of purple ribbons, including

a sequinned one, and left the ends long, like streamers. This is a demure, dainty and delightful little posy

that makes no apologies for being anything other than *utterly pretty and feminine*.

# Jewelled

Sumptuous effects can be achieved by mixing rich and glowing colours in a bridal bouquet. Opulent combinations – deepest purple and sunflower yellow, or vivid orange, maroon and shocking pink – can look magnificent if composed with thought and care.

Using different colours with the same intensity of tone and playing off warm against cool will keep a sense of balance. Adding a touch of white or a paler colour also prevents vibrant schemes from becoming garish.

These loose bouquets have a feeling of *natural abundance*.

The large, black-centred *poppy anemones* (*Anemone coronaria* De Caen) are available in a range of glowing jewel colours and are a welcome sight in flower markets in the darkest days of winter and early spring. Their wide open blooms have a cheerful charm.

Here, anemones are used as the centrepiece of an arrangement with a distinctly Pre-Raphaelite effect. The bride and bridesmaid's loose hair and simple dresses emphasize the *lush richness* of the loosely formed bouquet, posy and lavish wreath.

The bright pink and purple anemones are balanced with lilac (*Syringa*) in a cooler shade to keep the scheme *soft and romantic*. Both bouquets are finished with a variety of lilac and purple ribbons. These arrangements are large, tied bunches, giving them an informal, loose form and a feeling of natural abundance.

There's a feeling of *festivity and fun* about this exuberant bouquet. It's composed of white-and-pink camellias (*Camellia*), lilac and deep purple sweet peas (*Lathyrus odoratus*), and pink and orange-to-lime green ranunculus (*Ranunculus asiaticus*). The finishing touch is a collar of burgundy net and multicoloured ribbons.

The fullness and size of the arrangement matches the overall richness of the scheme, and the end result is a bouquet with a real *sense of theatre*. Handling clashing combinations such as orange and pink requires skill – here a delicate balance has been maintained by adding paler and darker colours: lilac, white and *deepest purple*.

A pretty evening bag makes an unexpected container for dainty pansies (*Viola* x *wittrockiana*) in shades of deep purple and golden yellow. Pansies are available from garden centres throughout the winter and spring months and come in *a dazzling array* of colours, including wine red, deep blue, bronze and even black – the bi-coloured varieties are particularly striking. Their petals have a luscious, velvety quality that is enhanced by these deep shades.

For this unusual arrangement with a hint of the *Twenties flapper*, three tiny posies have been tucked into the bag and secured to the straps. Other small flowers could be used in place of pansies, such as miniature, patio or spray roses (*Rosa*), sweet peas (*Lathyrus odoratus*) or poppy anemones (*Anemone coronaria* De Caen), all of which can be found in vibrant shades.

These three little raffia-tied *nosegays*
demonstrate another effective way of working with
strong colour. Rather than creating a mixed scheme, each
tightly packed posy uses ranunculus (*Ranunculus asiaticus*) in a
single colour, surrounded by a ruff of galax (*Galax*) leaves. *Cerise,*
*orange and maroon* are colours that work well together because they all share
red undertones. Ranunculus, with their exquisitely intricate form, have a long period of
availability, from the beginning of the year until early summer and then again in the
autumn. They also last extremely well when cut.

*A rainbow of roses* (Rosa) in luscious jewel shades has been used to create this opulent bouquet. Blue Curiosa (mauve), Illios (gold), Decca (tangerine), Lollipop (pale apricot) and Martinique (deep red) roses are offset with camellia (*Camellia*) foliage. Fine wire has been coiled around the bouquet to create a spun-sugar effect, with a lavender and gold ribbon to finish.

The result is quirky and fun, an unconventional approach to wedding flowers. Such a bold *mélange of dazzling colours* can be difficult to handle and requires an experienced eye. The shades used here are rich but not garish and there's a balance of cool and warm colours, ensuring that the flowers complement each other rather than clash.

# Dramatic

Boldly contrasting combinations make a strong statement. All colours can be paired up with their opposite, or complementary, colour and combinations of these create vivid effects – think of yellow and purple, blue and orange, or red and green.

White or cream can be used as a foil for deeper shades, such as ruby red or, most graphically of all, black. Such theatrical colour schemes are not for the faint-hearted but when handled with confidence they can produce undeniably spectacular results.

*Snow-white* and aubergine arum lilies (*Zantedeschia aethiopica*) are a sophisticated colour combination for an adventurous bride. This sheaf of them has been made even more dramatic by the addition of steel grass (*Xanthorrea australis*), whose thin blades emphasize the length of the lilies.

Arums have a strong *sculptural presence*, creating a bouquet with great elegance and poise. They were an Art Deco favourite, the perfect foil for that era's sinuous bias-cut gowns. This arrangement would look stunning carried by a twenty-first century bride in *a slim, satin gown*.

A *sophisticated* colour combination for an *adventurous* modern bride.

The most *dramatic* colour scheme of all is black and white. The combination may sound distinctly unbridal but this arrangement proves that it can be given a romantic treatment.

Striking white poppy anemones (*Anemone coronaria* De Caen) with an emphatic black 'eye' are combined with *dark wine* Black Beauty roses (*Rosa*), ranunculus (*Ranunculus asiaticus*) and galax (*Galax*) leaves. There is much delicacy of texture here, in the feathery stamens and silky petals of the anemones, the velvety rose petals and the closely furled ranunculus. Black and gold ribbon adds *a note of glamour*.

This dramatic yet *dreamy* bouquet would be an ideal choice for a winter wedding by *candlelight*.

In the cool light of midwinter the contrast between dark and light colours works wonderfully well. Red and white is *a classic combination* that seems just right for the season. It's an elegant partnership but also a dramatic one, particularly when teamed with the deep, forest greens of *winter foliage*.

This ravishing bouquet takes a slightly softer approach by using Anne-Marie roses (*Rosa*), which are a warm cream rather than pure white. They've been mingled with ruby red Martinique, Nicole and Grand Prix roses, whose blue undertones suit the wintry light, and skimmia (*Skimmia*), laurustinus (*Viburnum tinus*) and ivy leaves and berries (*Hedera helix*).

This *daring bouquet* takes a starkly modern approach and shows how flower arranging can cross over into the realms of sculpture. Painter's palette (*Anthurium*), with its thick and glossy petals, has been used for its *exotic and architectural* good looks. Partnering these tropical flowers are folded aspidistra (*Aspidistra*) leaves and hollow snake grass (*Scirpus tabernaemontani*) bent into angular shapes. Finally, soldering wire has been looped over the head of the bouquet and wrapped around its stem. The result is dramatic and uncompromising, an arrangement for a bride who likes to be different.

A Naranja rose set in a ruffle of burnt orange cockscomb with a green ribbon-bound stem. Accompanies the bouquet on pages 50-51.

A Bianca rose sits above gold-sprayed willow catkins. Skimmia leaves provide a finishing touch. Accompanies the bouquet on pages 28-29.

A silvery sprig of aromatic rosemary adorned with a flourish of coppery-brown striped ribbon. Accompanies the bouquet on page 95.

Above Martinique roses turned inside out and wrapped in galax. See pages 60-61. Below A Grand Prix rose, winter jasmine, rose leaves and cranberry ribbon. See page 59.

Grape hyacinths gathered in a ruff of galax leaves and tied with narrow navy-blue ribbon. Accompanies the bouquet on page 86.

An unfurled green and pink parrot tulip sheathed in a tulip leaf and studded with a pearl pin. Accompanies the bouquet on page 106.

Above left *Hyacinth florets secured with navy ribbon and a pearl pin. See page 88.*

Above centre *An Illios rose twinned with variegated pittosporum leaves. See pages 44-45.*

Above right *Scented cream sweet peas finished with purple sequinned trim. See pages 108-109.*

Below *A Candy Bianca rose set in ivy with rosebud braid decorating the stem. See pages 64-65.*

# buttonholes

Tradition has it that the *groom's buttonhole* should be plucked from the bride's bouquet to symbolize the fact that they will share everything in their *new life together*. The idea doesn't have to be followed literally, but all the buttonholes worn by the men in the bridal party (groom, best man, ushers and often fathers of the bride) should in some way echo the flowers used in the bride's bouquet. Extra interest can be added to the arrangements by *using scented blooms* (a buttonhole is situated in exactly the right place to be smelt by its wearer), interesting foliage and 'dressing' the stem in creative ways, such as with ribbon and pearl-headed pins.

# index

## publisher's acknowledgments

The publishers would like to thank everyone who assisted with the photography for this book.

Mike and Kumeko Paul, James and Rebecca Harris, Annie and Robin Munro-Davies, Jonathan and Camilla Ross, Kimberley Watson and Ros Fairman kindly allowed us to photograph in their homes.

Belair House Restaurant and Bar, The Chancery Court Hotel, The Phoenix Restaurant, The Savile Club, Mayfair and The Skin Rejuvenation Clinic, London generously allowed us to photograph on their premises.

The wedding gowns and bridesmaids' dresses were loaned by Virgin Bride, Berkertex Brides, Caroline Castigliano, Monsoon and Nicole Farhi. Many thanks to Joanne Souch at Virgin Bride for all her assistance.

Thanks are also due to all the little models, who made such beautiful bridesmaids, and to their parents for allowing them to take part.

Berkertex Brides
01476 593311
Branches nationwide

Caroline Castigliano
62 Berners Street
London W1T 3NQ
020 7636 8212

Nicole Farhi
158 New Bond Street
London W1Y 2PA
020 7499 8368
and branches nationwide

Monsoon
020 7313 3000
Branches nationwide
www.monsoon.co.uk

Virgin Bride
The Grand Buildings
Northumberland Avenue
London WC2N 5EJ
020 7321 0866
www.virginbride.co.uk

Belair House
Restaurant & Bar
Gallery Road
Dulwich Village
London SE21 7AB
020 8299 9788
fax: 020 8299 6793
email: belairhouse@aol.com
www.belairhouse.com

The Phoenix Restaurant
162-164 Lower Richmond Road
London SW15 1LY
020 8780 3131

Renaissance London Chancery Court Hotel
252 High Holborn
London WC1V 7EN
020 7829 9888
fax: 020 7829 9889
www.renaissancehotels.com

Jane Durbridge can be contacted at:
janedurbridge@parterre-flowers.co.uk

## *Author's acknowledgments*

I'd like to thank everyone who helped make my first book project such an enjoyable experience. Especially Stephen, my husband, who as a literary agent cajoled and encouraged me from start to end, and put up with interrupted nights when I woke in the wee small hours with some idea or another. Thank you also Mark and Claire, for family support.

The project was made great fun by a great team. Craig Fordham produced photographs beyond my wildest dreams, with imagination, verve and humour, and Rob, his assistant, kept Craig and the rest of us entertained and amused. Antonia Swinson gently extracted all the necessary information and made sure it appeared in the text. Thanks are due to the team at RPS: to Kate Brunt, who came visiting and found great locations, to Vicky Holmes, for all her help foraging for clothes and props and keeping us all fed and watered, and to Alison Starling, who took time and trouble to guide and offer advice and encouragement from the start. Above all, thanks go to Gabriella Le Grazie, for always being so enthusiastic and positive, despite the appalling weather that prevailed throughout the photography, and for designing such an imaginative and 'different' book on bridal bouquets.

A big thank you is due to Patsie, for being there and supplying odd cuppas or a glass of wine; to Isla, who was one of the first to goad me into taking up the challenge and for her family wedding, which was the start of it all; and to Christine and Martina for phone support. Thank you especially to Nigel, Nellie and the rest of the Parterre team, for holding the fort in my absence. I am enormously grateful to all the friends who opened their homes to us: James and Rebecca Harris, Annie and Robin Monro-Davies and Mike and Kumeko Paul, Nicholas Storey at the Savile Club, the management of the Chancery Lane Hotel, to Belair House Restaurant and Bar in Dulwich, and to Skin London.

Finally, a big kiss to all the beautiful little 'bridesmaids': Arianna, Niamh, Rita, Shannon and Stella.

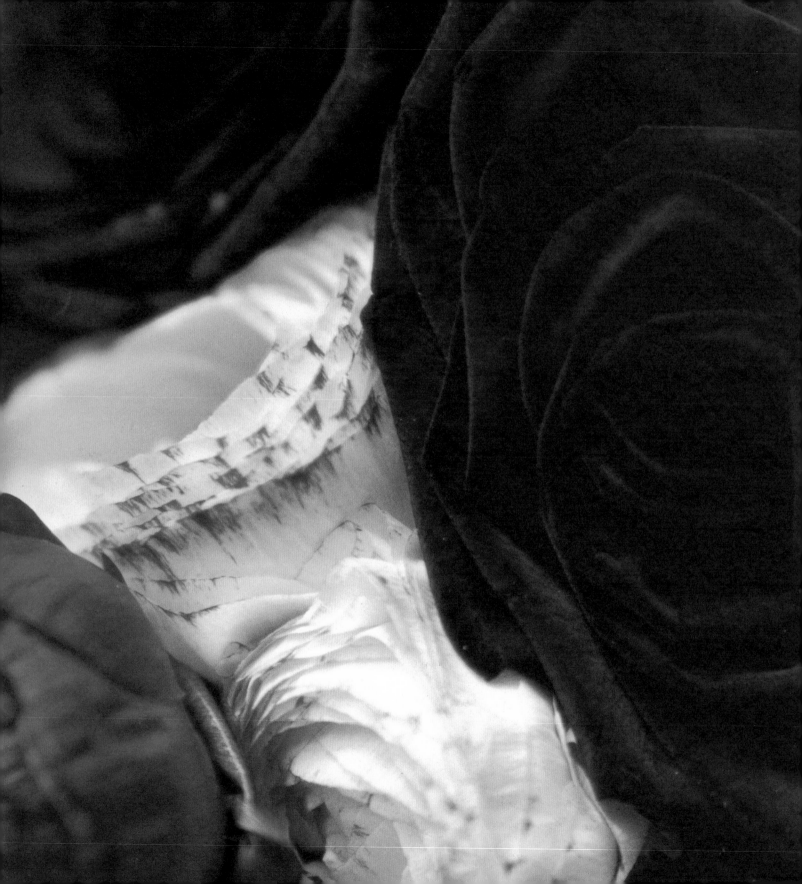